# Entrepreneurship

## Swift Sailing from Flat Broke to Treasure Island (Even in a Terrible Economy)

## John S. Rhodes

# Entrepreneurship

## Swift Sailing from Flat Broke to Treasure Island (Even in a Terrible Economy)

# Table of Contents

# FREE BONUS:
# Investment Strategies
# to Grow Your Income

Thank you for purchasing this book! As an added bonus, copy this link into your browser on your computer or tablet: http://jjfast.com/getrich/

You can then download a free bonus report that will show you...

- How to Choose the Perfect Passive Income Investment in 17 Minutes or Less

- Discover smart strategies that grow your portfolio yet actually still lower your investment risk

- See how to outpace inflation while growing wealth... but still get a reliable stream of income

- Learn about the best investment tactics that are guaranteed by the government

Just go to http://jjfast.com/getrich/ to access your free bonus!

# Prologue: Entrepreneurship in Context

A lot of people are disgusted by the rich. They're irritated. Folks are exasperated, disgruntled and just plain "pissed off" at the very wealthy. Demons! Burn them! Now, with that in mind, here's a weird question: Wouldn't it be far better for you to become as "filthy rich" as they are – yes, join them! – while also doing good for the world, sharing your dreams, and delivering massive value to others? In other words, wouldn't it be better to...

**...have your cake, and eat it too.**
**(Yes Virginia, there is a Santa Claus!)**

No kidding, we'll get there. This is not a fantasy. There's a proven strategy that anyone can use. It's called entrepreneurship and we will dig into that shortly. But first, we've got to start by understanding all the rage against the rich. We've got to understand what's really going on and why so many people feel cheated. We've got briefly look at the trends and some very basic data. So, let's get going...

The tide of opinion throughout the first world, and particularly in the United States, has been hammering steadily and fiercely against the so-called "1%." The destruction of trust after the housing market crash, Occupy Wall Street, the congressional fiscal deadlocks, and the creation of the terms "99%" and "1%" have created a powerful Us-vs-Them climate. The popular perception is that the very wealthy are at best out of touch, most often condescending and apathetic, and at worst malevolent robber-barons determined to crush the middle-class beneath their luxurious stiletto heels and line their pockets with the blood, sweat and tears of the poor. No doubt, there are corrupt people who have earned their fortunes dishonestly and harmfully, or never lifted a finger and were simply born into wealth.

However, this is dead wrong. Let's pull back the curtain. Like my friend Jeff Walker, I believe that entrepreneurs will save the world. Here's the reason why:

**4 out of 5 millionaires created and developed their wealth the old-fashioned, proven way: by creating value for others.** They did not steal their money, or beg their parents for it. They did not exploit or take advantage of people less fortunate than themselves. They embrace entrepreneurship. It's true that these wealthy people are sometimes the high-profile people in our culture, the celebrities, sports stars, and CEO's of multi-billion dollar companies. Most of the 1% is not so well-known, but they are still superstars. They are normal people on a mission. They provide products, services, and information so valuable and good that customers can't help but buy them. They are carpet cleaners, self-published authors and freelance graphic artists. **They are entrepreneurs.**

These people are not superhuman. They are not born with silver spoons in their mouths and they don't have magic powers. That's good news because it means that just about anyone can become part of the 1%, and do it in as little as 3 years.

**This book will show you how to become rich, using the practices, ideas, and secrets that the superstars use, and do so without selling your soul to the devil.** You do not need to be selfish, mean or nasty to become wealthy. In fact, you need to exhibit positive qualities, and the most important one of all is a sincere desire to help other people. You also need to understand the habits of wealth.

This book will not teach you a simple magic trick to become instantly wealthy. It will not make becoming rich easy. But, if you are willing to work, and you are willing to be a little patient, this book gives you the ultimate foundation of success. It will change the way you think about money, business, capitalism, and ambition. Further, it will give you the vital information that you need to become part of the 1%. You can become quite wealthy and have a blast at the same time. In other words, this book will show you how to build wealth with integrity, and let you keep your soul. **It's the golden path of entrepreneurship.**

# Who Are the 1%?

The "top 1%" of Americans, for most practical purposes, are the very wealthy. In strict terms, the percentile refers to highest income bracket in America. In 1979, a person needed to earn at least $165,000 a year to be part of the 1%. In 1989, the income cut-off point was $217,000. As of 2007, a person's annual income needed to be about $350,000. By now it's as high as $400,000.

$400,000 per year is enough to live like royalty. But you don't need to earn a 1%'ers income to become wealthy. It is important to recognize that **being wealthy is not the same thing as having a lot of income.** Many millionaire entrepreneurs earn as little as $100,000 a year. On the flip side, consider how many celebrities and sports stars earn millions of dollars a year and yet are constantly struggling financially.

**True wealth is about what you keep, not what you earn.**

There is an undeniable gap between the top 1% earners and the 99%, many of whom earn less than $30,000 a year. The massive inequality in income is a well-known and serious problem.

But, get this mind blowing fact –

The simple existence of inequality is a good thing. The bizarre truth is that inequality is what makes capitalism work. Better yet, as the inequality grows, the opportunities for great success also grow. Best of all, you can use those opportunities. **Inequality is how superstar entrepreneurs make money**.

# Inequality in Wealth But True Equality in Entrepreneurial Opportunity

Consider the ultimate example of income and lifestyle equality: communism. Communism is a system made with good intentions. Everyone gets what they need. Everyone can contribute something to the common good. Everyone is equal.

**Equally mediocre, that is.**

In a communist society, there is no incentive for anyone to excel. No matter how hard you work, you get the same as everyone else. You only have a chance of getting ahead by getting some sort of governing position, or getting special favors, etc. Every way to better your lot is a corruption of the system.

One of the truly valuable traits of capitalism is that **those who work with the**

**system can do better for themselves**. In capitalism, doing well does not mean you are beating the system, it means you are using the system correctly. Capitalism works incredibly well for entrepreneurs because there is inequality: room for some to do better than average, and consequently, room for others to do worse than average.

Without that inequality, there is no opportunity.

Yet while there is inequality in outcomes, our system is open for entry by anyone. It's true beyond argument that circumstances such as poverty, ignorance, and regrettably, physical aspects that make people unique can make it harder to succeed. However, these obstacles can be overcome, and the capitalist system is impartial to these differences. Anyone can make it work: there is no government magistrate that rips the cash from your hands as soon as you earn it. **Everyone has the opportunity to try to succeed as an entrepreneur.**

It is not wrong, bad or evil to be successful. You have the same opportunity anyone has: to try to become wealthy. If you step up and try, your chances are a lot better than you might think.

Superstars need inequality to do what they do best: generate value. In order to become wealthy, you need to generate value too. By creating great value, you'll make a ton of money, and you'll quickly understand why the income gap has gotten as extreme as it has: **entrepreneurial superstars are generating a *lot* of value.**

(That's how they get joyfully rich!)

However, simply making money is not enough if your money burns away as soon as you get it. Becoming wealthy requires a certain mindset about money and wealth. Let's explore why income and wealth are not the same.

And, if you have the right mindset, you can enjoy far greater wealth. Keep reading to understand why **focus and attention radically improve your odds**.

# What You See Is What You Get

As noted earlier, it is equally possible to make only a little money in income and become fantastically wealthy. Likewise, you can make a ton of money yet have no real wealth. A person earning $1,000,000 a year will still burn through their money very quickly if they are blind about where their money goes. What you see if what you get: **if you see where your money goes, you will keep more of it.**

Most people focus on their income, always trying to make more each year. This is not wrong. In fact, it's brilliant. But, most people do not pay proper attention to the money that they already have. It's a law of nature: What you focus on tends to grow, and what you neglect tends to shrink. Consider playing the violin: if you focus on playing the violin, practicing everyday, you will get better and better. If you stop practicing, then your skills deteriorate.

Money works the same way for entrepreneurs: **If you do not focus on the money that you have, then your money and your business dies.** Harsh, but true.

Simply placing your money in the bank is neglecting your money, and it will literally die on you. Savings accounts carry interest rates below inflation: money sitting neglected in the bank loses buying power every day. Money sitting in a sack under your bed loses even more buying power. You do not need to spend money to lose money, because when it sits idle, it slowly but surely disappears. This is always true when inflation is greater than the interest you earn.

What do the wealthy entrepreneurs do? Simple! They track their business net worth and their personal net worth. It's so simple yet so powerful. To say it another way: All wealthy people track their net worth on a regular basis... because they know that what they focus on will grow. Here's how to do it starting right now:

Net worth is everything you own, minus everything you owe: your assets minus your liabilities. Be strict about which is which, stricter than standard accounting practices may have taught you. Count assets only as things that make money for you, or money itself. Count liabilities as anything that drains money away from you, such as your car. When you make it a habit to track your net worth, you will start to feel pressure to gain more assets and cut expenses.

It's like a law of nature: **Your net worth – your true wealth – will begin to grow, if all you do is pay attention to it.** This increases the pleasure you get from your money and it also increases your pain when you waste it. It's the good old carrot and stick, applied to your money and it's what wealthy, successful entrepreneurs do. Focus and attention create a wealthy mindset and growth opportunities for entrepreneurs.

## How to Enjoy Income Taxes

It's no secret that the higher your income, the more you lose to taxes. Income tax is a way of redistributing wealth. But remember: **being wealthy is not about income alone**. If you fight against taxes, you will lose in the end. Here's why...

Getting rich is not about beating the tax system. It's great to pay 2-3% less tax on the money you make. So, minimize your taxes legally and responsibly. Really, that's the smart thing to do. However, wealthy entrepreneurs people don't myopically focus on minimizing their income taxes because they know that income taxes are only a minor irritant in the grand scheme. **Taxes suck, but it's far more important to focus on growing income.**

Ask yourself this question: Are you more likely to get rich by making more money, or by saving money through tax minimization? The answer is by making more money. Next, consider this analogy: Will you have more apples to eat if you pick an additional apple from the tree, or if you put lemon juice on one apple to preserve it longer? (Lemon juice preserves apples, if you didn't know.)

Or, using simple math... if your tax rate is 30%, then you still get to keep $0.70 on every additional dollar you generate. On the flip side, if you can knock your taxes down to 25% from 30%, that's only $0.05 of extra money. If you're like most entrepreneurs, you will instantly recognize that focusing on making $0.70 more on every dollar is much smarter than focusing on saving $0.05 on every dollar. The rich and powerful get this. It's why they focus on growth. And therefore, that's where you will find truth behind successful businesses. **This is an abundance mindset.**

# Educate Yourself

Entrepreneurs prize education. However, not all education is created equal. Formal education, such as what you get with high school diploma, a bachelor's or master's degree, or even a PhD, is certainly useful in a lot of ways. It opens doors and opportunities for you. It impresses people. It shows that you are able to concentrate, work with authority figures, complete assignments, and manage your time. It teaches you good practices and gives you loads of facts that can be useful, or depending on the occupation, vitally necessary. Formal education is nice, safe, and generally quite boring.

**Formal education is pleasant and useful, but self-education is the "special sauce" that you really need... to ENJOY entrepreneurship.**

Superstars develop a thirst for self-education, becoming lifelong learners. There is a lot of information that can be translated directly into wealth, and this information can't be learned in school. The 1% carefully study: the daily demands of running a business; about niche's likes, dislikes, needs and fears; how to sell and market in a niche; and the latest technology and techniques of the trade. All of this can only be learned through self-education, by reading magazines and books, talking to people, working, trying new things, making mistakes, and gaining experience. In fact, it's absolutely necessary to soak yourself in a bath of this kind of business content from time to time. It's refreshing!

Superstar entrepreneurs are learning machines that pick up knowledge and make the most of it. They get to learn a little bit of everything, but they don't need to know EVERYTHING about everything. Instead, they focus on their unique abilities, and they find people that have unique abilities too. **The**

**secret is that the wealthy create teams where each person maximizes their top 2-3 talents.** The focus is on maximizing strength, not fixing weaknesses. Ironically, this is exactly the opposite of what we're formally taught in school... where you're mostly punished for failure.

## How You Can Be a Superstar Entrepreneur

I've been throwing around the word "superstar" for a little while now, and you might be wondering: **"What is a superstar entrepreneur?"**

A superstar is just an ordinary person with a few traits, and a few habits, that make them exceptional. You can express these traits and learn these habits. Superstars do the right things, mostly the small stuff, again and again. 1%'ers rarely strike it rich overnight. It can take a few years, or many years.

You have already learned a few of the most important habits: tracking your wealth, investing your wealth, and relentlessly self-educating. All you have to do is practice these habits and the others shown to you in this book, and you'll be halfway there!

I'll put it another way. You already possess the traits of a superstar entrepreneur... all you have to do is start expressing them. Superstars are not workaholics, geniuses, brilliant creatives, or stunningly ambitious people. They are just good people; people like you. Most importantly, they focus on the value they provide to others, and they stay focused no matter what.

Superstars are reliable and respectful. They are willing to work hard doing something they love. They are open-minded and thoughtful. They are focused, above all, on delivering what people want. They are happy to do it! And, above all, **superstars are entrepreneurs, because entrepreneurs are flesh-n-blood value creation machines.**

You already have everything you need inside of you to be a superstar, so all that's left is to practice a few basic, boring, but important habits. When you have them down-pat, you will become wealthy, slowly but surely.

Then again, you don't want to wait forever, do you? If you want to get that wealth in the fastest, most reliable way possible, then read on...

## Your Greatest Asset (Besides You)

Practicing those basic, boring habits will put you in the superstar's mindset. The best way to apply that shiny new mindset is to start a business. Starting a business is how most wealthy people become wealthy. Having your own business will give you the power to earn as much as you want to make.

**Your greatest asset, besides you... is your business.**

There are two things that you need to successfully start a business: great tenacity, and sufficient capital. Most businesses do not fail from one more often than the other, because they are both very important. Most fledgling business owners simply underestimate how much they need of both; they do not know what it takes to attain "Escape Velocity."

The goal of every business is to reach that escape velocity, to reach a point of no return where things just about take care of themselves. Actually getting to that point is extremely challenging. The "gravitational pull" against your business is really incredible. People will tell you that you can't succeed, delays and problems will constantly arise, crises will emerge, expenses will sneak up on you, competition will fight you, and the pure toil of spending time on the books and the nitty-gritty details can wipe out your motivation and your passion. You need a huge amount of tenacity to not give up against all of the challenges as an entrepreneur.

You also need the capital to back up your guts. Bootstrapping and improvising can only get you so far before you have to commit real resources, and the amount of money required to get a business all the way to escape velocity is much more than the amount needed to simply start. If you run out of cash even a hair's breadth before you break free, you will fall back to earth. It's as simple as that. Your business's cash is like blood: if it runs dry, your business dies. But, there's a "trick" that great entrepreneurs use, and that you can borrow... **The most successful businesses are the ones that generate the most cash on the lowest investment.**

What kinds of businesses do not require much cash?

Service businesses generally don't need much cash to get started and keep going. Cleaning services, freelancing services, coaching and teaching services: these sorts of businesses can be started up with know-how, a fistful of cash, and maybe a business license.

Just think about what you can provide that's valuable to others, then figure out how to deliver it to customers. When you can do that, you have a business. It's that simple.

# Find the Millionaires in Your Market

Your business needs to exist in a niche that you are comfortable and familiar with, and one that can support even more businesses. Learn everything you can about that niche, figuring out what people fear and desire the most; this invaluable information will help you deliver the most value to that niche. Also, start digging. Find out who's "filthy rich" in your market. Unless you are in a truly peculiar niche, such as underwater basket weaving, then there are millionaires in your market.

Find them!

These millionaire entrepreneurs probably will not be like the A-List celebrities. They are not Michael Jordans, Brad Pitts, and Katy Perrys. They won't be chauffeured in limos; they'll drive decent-to-good cars. They won't live in a castle. They might go to church, or be a part of their local PTA. Most millionaires are surprisingly regular people, but they are absolutely focused on creating value for their markets.

Because those millionaires are so much like ordinary people, they are not often explicitly seen or heard in their markets. Instead, **they are felt in their markets**. They are felt through their products and services. Truly titanic businesses, such as Apple, are seen and heard because their market impact is like huge earthquakes. When Apple releases a new i-Something, consumers line up in droves to get at it. All that matters is this...

Find your niche millionaires, **then copy what they do**.

You will find that these 1%'ers work only a little bit harder than non-millionaires who are supporting themselves comfortably. If the average person works 40 hours a week, millionaires are working more like 45-50. You don't need to exhaust yourself with 80-90 hour work weeks; you only need to work a little bit more. (Well, except when you first get started.) This is one of the key habits of a superstar: working just a little bit harder. As the great Napoleon Hill said many times, **"Go the extra mile."**

You will also find that the superstar entrepreneurs in your niche are following a foolproof formula. They have found a niche that needs something (an opportunity), they are focused on their customer's needs 100%, they provide real value to those customers, and they practice basic boring business habits like tracking their wealth.

Now, do the math to prove the truth to yourself:

+ **Opportunity**

+ **Customer Focus**

+ **Creating Value**

+ **Habits**

= **MILLIONAIRE**

Copy the successful entrepreneurs in your niche, and you will succeed, too.

# Don't Start From Scratch, Do This Instead

While you emulate the habits and practices of millionaires, your business should also emulate other successful businesses. To put it another way, **it is much harder to succeed through radical innovation than it is through emulation and improvement**.

Consider Apple. Many think of Apple as a radically innovative company, but in fact, they do a lot of emulation. Their iPod is often considered a brand-new idea, but there were plenty of MP3 players on the market before Apple released the iPod, and some of those MP3 players were technically superior. Apple came up with specific innovations and improvements: they created a user interface that was intuitive to even the least technology-savvy, they created a brand of customer service to go along with it, and they marketed it extremely well.

**Don't radically innovate. Relentlessly adjust and improve on what works!**

You don't need to create a brand-new product out of thin air because that's difficult and very risky to do so. Of course, you don't want to just rip off someone else's idea and slap your name on it. Customers know what a rip-off looks like, and worst case scenario it's illegal and you'll find yourself with a lawsuit or worse. Instead, find what people want, emulate the basics, and improve on what needs improving. Add your special sauce! Let your improvements and your targeted but unique ideas create something special. You'll deliver the most value to your market this way, and the profits that you reap will prove that is true.

# Build an Entrepreneurial Team

Every entrepreneur should know a little bit about everything in their niche, and a little about everything that makes a business run well. That said, everyone has their own talents, preferences, education, and expertise, and working with those talents is the best way to succeed. Doing everything yourself is inefficient at best, self-destructive at worst.

**Trying to do everything... leaves you with nothing.**

You need to create a team. The most basic team is the classic partnership of two minds, one keeping an eye on the day-to-day basics such as keeping the books, the other on creating and selling the product. One person simply can't run a successful business by themselves, so you must find people that complement your strengths and weaknesses.

Your first inclination will be to find teammates you can trust, and this will naturally lead you to friends and family. But, here's a warning: Trust alone is not enough to create a successful business team. It's a sad truth that many new businesses have failed because they were composed of friends and family. You may trust your best friend with your life, but they may not have the skills the business needs to succeed. **In a successful entrepreneurial business, what matters is that people can do their job well.** Of course, if they are really cool, that's a huge bonus.

# Entrepreneurs Succeed by Maximizing Their Productivity

Jean-Baptiste Say remarked: **"An entrepreneur is someone who takes resources from a lower level to a higher level of productivity."** In other words, the best entrepreneurs get the most output out of their inputs: they feed coal into their businesses and end up with diamonds.

You need to minimize your inputs and maximize your outputs, and there are several ways to do this. The first is to use the best raw materials that you possibly can: the highest quality, most available stuff that you can properly afford. If you're in the business of making cell phones, then you want the best cell phone parts you can get. Do the best you can, while keeping in mind that the most expensive materials are not necessarily the best.

Remember that your primary goal is to deliver value to your customers. If you are selfish about your business, focusing on your raw passion and what you really want to make, **then you are not creating value for others**.

This is the critical difference between artists and entrepreneurs: an artist creates something for its own sake, and they create precisely what they want to create regardless of what other people want. The best artists accept that others may not value what they create.

As an entrepreneur, **your success or failure is defined by the value others place in your creations.** Through good marketing, you can convince others that what you make is valuable, but you will meet the most success by creating the most valuable products that you can. To do otherwise is to try to work against the system, and it will not go the way you want it to.

Consider if you are going to play in a football game: What is the smartest thing you can do? If you bring a baseball team onto the field, and try to play baseball to beat a football team at football, then you will have a terrible time and will probably lose. That's what it's like to try to work against the system.

If you really want to win the game, then you need to work with the system. You get together the best football team that you can, with the best players for each position trained by the best coaches. You come up with a game plan, and then you play football.

Delivering the most value to your customers, and using the most efficient materials and processes, is the game of business. When you play the game right, you might lose, or you might win, but if you will absolutely lose if you play the game wrong. **Entrepreneurs give people what they want.**

# Market, Market, Market

No matter how good your product is, it can't walk off a store shelf and crawl into a customer's house, then put money into your bank account. If you create a wonderful product and keep it secret in your house, no one will ever buy it. You have to market your product, and yourself, as much as possible. Marketing is key!

How should you think about selling? Is it wicked, evil or dirty? Hell no! Here's the best definition of selling that I've ever seen. It's powerful. Read this slowly and carefully to get maximum value:

**"Selling is getting someone intellectually engaged in a future result that is good for them and getting them to emotionally commit to take action to achieve that result."**

~ Dan Sullivan

Good marketing complements a good product. You need to get the word out, and you need to be noticed despite the millions upon millions of others people also trying to get noticed. Your marketing has got to engage people, it's got to be good for them, it's got to get them emotionally involved, and they have to take action. That's the secret.

The internet provides some powerful tools for exposure: blogs, social media, press releases, email lists, forums, podcasts, web videos! The internet is chock full of powerful marketing options, and many of them are free or extremely cheap to use. Emotionally connect and get folks to take action for their own good, so that they achieve what they want to achieve, so that they get what they really need.

Traditional methods also still have power. Direct mailing has met with success for decades and still can do work. Going to tradeshows, whether as an attendee or as a presenter, can help you network with other professionals in your niche and interact directly with your ideal customers. A magazine article, radio interview, or television spot can never hurt, if you can put together the contacts and resources to make them happen, but you don't need to resort to such expensive saturation marketing to succeed.

**What's the entrepreneurial secret of marketing success? It's testing.** No matter what product your selling, or how you're selling it, the secret to growing your business, making money and creating foam-at-the-mouth fans is through testing. For every $1 dollar invested, find a way to generate $1.01 or more. Then, just keep reinvesting once your data shows you to the true path.

Marketing lets your customers get to know your product, and helps you get to know your customers. It's a symbiosis! You and your customers are actually partners. By carefully tracking your marketing successes and failures, you will get a better idea of what your customers like and dislike, and then you can make even better products and market them even more efficiently. There's no doubt about it, communication is the rocket fuel that the filthy rich love to use. That because...

**"Markets Are Conversations"**

~ The Cluetrain Manifesto

The bottom line is that you should never pass up an opportunity to do more marketing and get more exposure. The more people that know you, the more people that can buy your product: A customer that you never meet is a customer that you will never get. **So, make yourself seen and heard at every opportunity!**

## Entrepreneurial Leverage

Once you have a great product, you can do more with it than simply sell it. Using a product for all of its potential is called leverage, and getting good leverage can make you filthy rich while doing a lot less work.

It's also a lot more fun!

**One method of leveraging is licensing**. Rather than outright selling your product, you can license it for a fee. This can give you leverage over the product through control of distribution: You still own the product, and are only selling the rights to use it by certain people in certain channels. Alternatively, you can license other people's products and then focus on distribution and marketing, leveraging the work of someone else to your gain. You can gain leverage on either side of the coin.

To replicate yourself and gain leverage, simply license your intellectual property. Your brainpower – for example, captured in an information product – can allow you to replicate yourself millions of times. Do you see how digital products, patents, and even children's books can multiply profits extremely fast? Intellectual properly and equity are so juicy!

Replication opportunities are everywhere and smoking hot entrepreneurial businesses "get" that. For example, at the most basic level, the internet is a distribution channel. Getting "yourself" and your brainpower online is easier than ever. Replication online is so easy... and that is leverage, my friend. As another example, software does not need to be remade every time it is sold: it is copied an unlimited number of times for free and the copies licensed or sold. Replicate and you gain leverage. Beautiful!

**Leverage your existing products to create new products**. If you write a giant book of short stories, don't just offer the compilation: separate the stories and sell them piecemeal on Kindle, and then cross promote them. It works like magic and it costs you nothing. Suddenly, you have a dozen products instead of just one. Or, let's flip this around. Gather up a bunch of books, or products, and offer them in various bundles. And, of course, to juice everything, simply create valuable but inexpensive bonuses for the products you create so that customers are even more interested in what you have to offer. Be creative!

**When you work with your products like this, you are engaging in a process like the fission and fusion of atoms and molecules. Break the big down into the small, build the small up into the big.** You are engaging in a very powerful and real kind of creation when you do this. And remember, this is what millionaires do. This is also why the filthy rich love information products, like electronic books and video training courses – because they are so easy to digitally manipulate and distribute. This is easy entrepreneurial leverage.

You can also leverage current technology to give yourself an advantage, either over your competition or simply to create and distribute better products to your customers. However, there is a catch to leveraging technology, one so important that it requires its own chapter...

# Entrepreneurs on the Cutting Edge... (Without Bleeding)

In order to get technical leverage, you need to be up to date on technology. The problem with technical leverage is that it rarely lasts long. It's like a sugar high; powerful but soon there's a crash. On the other hand, leverage from new products, new ways of selling products, or leverage gained from exceptional employees or partners, cannot be easily taken away. In any event, technical leverage is gradually eroded, because technology is generally meant to be available. It gets out there fast **but there is decay**.

Consider the Ford Motor Company: Their automated assembly line gave them incredible technical leverage and additional profits, for a while. After a few years others were able to copy how it worked and make their own assembly lines, quickly destroying Ford's early technical advantage.

**Technical leverage is powerful, but temporary**.

That is why entrepreneurs must always be on the cutting edge. Be ready and open to learn about new ideas, new products, and anything that can help you get an edge. Constant change can feel uncomfortable, but it is something that you must overcome and embrace. Stay on the pulse, and stay red hot. **You cannot fall behind the times.**

Although you need to be on top of current technology, you do not necessarily have to master the ins and outs of the technology in order to use it. For example, you do not really need to know how a microprocessor works in order to use a laptop. Mastery of something is required to change and repair, but not to use. Learn what you need to learn to use the latest stuff, and don't worry about learning more. The filthy rich understand that **you do not need to be an**

**expert to be on the cutting edge.**

(Although...rumor has it that billionaire Warren Buffett *still* doesn't use email.)

# Spot Trends and Use Them

Keeping your finger on the pulse of technology matters, but keeping your finger on the pulse of the market matters substantially more. People's tastes, needs, wants, and fears change over time. Tracking trends is how you stay ahead of the market and deliver the products your customers value the most, every time, year after year. This is an entrepreneurial truth.

You can't look into a crystal ball to discover trends, so what can you do? If you are constantly self-educating, then you will naturally notice trends all on your own. That's great: Remember that when you focus on something, you improve it. Focus on "trend hunting," and you'll get better at spotting what really matters.

There's an even better way to do it. And, this is what 1%'ers do all the time, through every channel possible. It this easy:

**Ask your customers what they want to see in your products.**

If you ask one customer, then you have a preference; if you ask ten, you'll notice a trend. Learn to love this data! You can even try asking your own team. They work with your products everyday, and they'll notice things and naturally be empathetic towards what your customers want. **If you want to find the hottest trend, just ask!**

By the way, the entrepreneurs know that there are two kinds of trends that matter: niche trends and macro trends. Spotting niche trends is pretty easy to do, especially if you are talking to your customers and observing them. An example of a niche trend is the proliferation of supernatural romance novels. Writers, publishers, and editors all likely anticipated this trend the moment that the *"Twilight"* series of supernatural romance books became a breakout success. The trend is so powerful that people outside the trend can observe it.

Trends that spread over culture are harder to spot, but are very valuable. Smaller trends tend to tell you want products to make. The supernatural romance trend informs authors that they should write those books, publishers that they should publish more of those books, etc.

**Now, what about macro-trends?**

Macro-trends show how products can be improved or changed, so those trends can provide you with a lot more leverage. A good example of a macro trend is the radical increase towards mobility. Mobile technology, such as smartphones and tablet devices, are simply the most lucrative forerunners of the trend of constant movement and accessibility to and from anything and everywhere. The mobility of the disabled has been improving too, with sophisticated robotic prosthetics and affordable, more mobile chairs. The greatest improvement to American infrastructure currently being debated is cross-country high-speed rail. Cloud systems make offices and information storage more mobile. Mobility is a macro trend that covers many industries.

Another trend is miniaturization. Everything is becoming smaller and smaller. Cell phones continue to shrink. MP3 players can be as small as a silver dollar. Smart cars are tiny, efficient, and becoming more popular by the day as gas prices rise. "Micro apartments" are now being sold in New York City. As the population continues to rise and resource management becomes more and more of a problem, miniaturization will cross into more and more industries.

You do not need to be a trendsetter (remember: innovation is risky), but you should find the trends and make them work for you. The goal is to create value, and trends will tell you what your customers find valuable. Great entrepreneurs know: **You don't have to be the tsunami itself, you**

**just need to ride the wave.**

## Entrepreneurship Success: Three EverGREEN Niches

There are thousands of niches, but some more lucrative than others. Some niches have been around for a long time, like automobile manufacture and repair. Some niches are on their way out, such as brick and mortar video rental stores or bookstores. Some niches are really only fads that flare up and die within a span of a year or two. There are three things that people will always care about however, and despite the huge numbers of entrepreneurs working in these special niches, there will always be room for you:

**1) Money**. Making money, keeping money, investing money, spending money...money is on the minds of everybody that uses it. People care a lot about money and they always will, because money can translate itself into so many other things.

**2) Health and Fitness**. Humans are animals after all, and while we may grow ever-more sophisticated and educated, we cannot escape our biological nature. Humans need to see, touch, hear, smell, and taste. They need to eat and excrete. They need to stay free of disease, and recover from it quickly. They need to keep fit. Anything having to do with health and fitness will always be able to make money, because everybody has to pay attention to it.

**3) Relationships**. Humans are social animals that need to interact with other humans. Humans are also very complex, and so their relationships constantly require maintenance and improvement. Whether it's raising a child, keeping friends happy, or trying to find a romantic partner, humans can't get enough advice about social issues. Of the three, this may be the single most powerful money-maker.

These topics will never go away, and will always serve you well. Money, health, and relationships: the golden triangle. **Technology is always replaced, trends go cold, and fads come and go, but people are people.**

# Entrepreneurship Zen: Become the Flow, Become Selfless

Your goal is to provide value to others. Do so honestly and enthusiastically.

**Hugely successful entrepreneurs provide ridiculous levels of value to others; *never forget!* There is karma in business, between you, your employees, your partners and your customers.**

When you sincerely work for the benefit of other people, you will find that success quite naturally comes to you. People recognize real value and desire it; if you create real value, then people will want you to stick around and continue delivering that value. **Value attracts value.** Superstar entrepreneurs are committed to helping people, and their reward is their ever-growing wealth.

People are very perceptive. Humans can tell if other humans don't really care about what they do, and when they are profiteering. Consider two home builders: one wants to make great houses for people, and the other just wants to make a lot of money. Even if the selfish home-maker pretends to be selfless, customers will easily notice that they're not: It will show up in their work, their habits, their interactions, and their demeanor. **As a superstar, your sincere desire to deliver value will drive you to make the best products and interact positively with your customers... and they will notice!**

Ask yourself: Who is hungry and desperate? Who has needs that are unfulfilled? Who really, really needs your help the most? Find out who those people are, and then figure out how to help them. Provide what they need with an honest smile and the satisfaction that you're doing something good. When you work like that, then you are being a true superstar. You are emulating the 1% by creating value for others this way. "Stinking rich" entrepreneurs are the most likely people to sell products and provide services to those who are hungry and desperate for solutions... And listen, aren't we *all* "hungry and desperate" from time to time? Stopping a divorce... Getting your ex back... losing weight fast to fit into a wedding dress... getting rid of wrinkles... making money fast to pay the bills... 1%'ers are providing solutions!

# Epilogue: Entrepreneurship is the Wealthy Choice

The growing income and wealth inequality gap in the world may be unjust. There are people who have gotten irrational sums of money by exploiting loopholes, exploiting people, and cheating. Most of the wealthy... the 1%'ers... the filthy rich... have earned their money by providing value to others and becoming superstar entrepreneurs. You can do the same, **but you have to make a choice.**

You can choose to fight the system and work to change the rules of the game. You can view inequality as something that can and should be blunted and destroyed by governments, corporations, or changes in culture. Rage against the machine! You can blame the 1% for causing the inequality, and demand that they redistribute their wealth. Grab the pitchforks...

**Or, you can join them. Embrace entrepreneurship.**

Listen, you have just gained extraordinary knowledge. You know how the 1%'ers created their wealth. You know *why* they are really so stupendously and insanely successful. They are predominantly entrepreneurs! You know how they view the world, their businesses and their money. Lastly, and most importantly, you know that you can do it to. Simple habits, slight mindset adjustments, focusing on others and their wants, and their needs. That's the life of wealthy entrepreneurs.

I'll end my time with you with this simple question...

**If you know that the casino always wins over time, why bet against the house when you can make your own casino? That's the entrepreneurial**

**secret.** It's how you can become fantastically wealthy, without selling your soul.

www.ingramcontent.com/pod-product-compliance
Lightning Source LLC
Chambersburg PA
CBHW071619170526
45166CB00003B/1120